BEAUTIFUL & FULL OF MONSTERS

COURTNEY LEBLANC

For (though not always about) Jay

Beautiful

"You're a storyteller. Dream up something wild and improbable," she pleaded. "Something beautiful and full of monsters."

"Beautiful and full of monsters?"

"All the best stories are."

~ from *Strange the Dreamer* by Laini Taylor

MONSTERS

FOREST FIRE

*In order to promote healthy growth, the National Park Service
periodically conducts controlled burns in Redwood forests.*

I have a Redwood growing
out of my chest, a towering mass
of bark and leaves, older
than a millennia. It reaches
toward sunlight, aches for water
and your touch.
I am too wild, too rugged
wilderness, too much. When you light
a match I lean toward the hiss
and pop. It climbs the dry bark,
racing to the top, leaves
and hair exploding in flame,
the colors lighting up the forest
inside me. You stand watching
me burn.

If Only

If only I hadn't been seventeen
and certain
I was ready to be an adult.
If only he hadn't been twenty-one
and unafraid
of the word *statutory*.
If only his friends had thought
I was off-limits.
If only they hadn't plied me
with beer and Southern Comfort.
If only my mother/father/sister/brother
had taught me my body wasn't
a commodity to trade.
If only I hadn't risen and fallen
like the stock market
with every touch – the crash
inevitable and foreseen
by everyone but me.
If only I hadn't equated
sex with love.
If only I knew I could say *no*
to a boy even if I'd say *yes*
to another.
If only his friends hadn't passed
me around
like a treat everyone wanted
to taste
but no one wanted to love.
If only sex didn't hold
the power I wanted
to wield.
If only my mouth had learned
to form the word *no*.

BUCKET HEART

You learned to play
the song of my (rib)cage,
clattered up the bones
that held my bucket heart,
filled in the gaps as best
you could.
The fissures that remained
couldn't hold against
the tsunami you kept
as a pet, the chaos
you couldn't control.
Once the storm surge
recedes
we'll see if my chalk-
colored bones remain,
we'll see if my bucket
heart has room
for you.

REWIND

I want to rewind
to the day we met, undo all the things
I've done. I want to take back that first
kiss – when you pressed me up against
the wall, ground your body into mine.
I want to take back the low growl
that escaped my lips, that told
you everything. I want to take
back your hot skin against
mine, the sheets wrapped
around us, your hand on my
hip – as if I hadn't pledged
myself to another. I want to take back
my lips on your skin, the frantic
phone calls, the secret texts.
I want to take back the discovery,
the words flying like buckshot – uncaring
where they landed but knowing they'd
hurt. I want to take back the fists
clenched, the jagged
pacing, the hole punched
in the wall. I want to take
back the ache inside me, the way
the word *yes* fell from my mouth.

SHELTER

His voice is a storm
I've learned to weather.
He lives in a state of tornado
watches and hurricane warnings.
The sun hidden by storm
clouds for so long my skin
has grown pale and translucent.
A ghost-girl growing cold,
my blue blood pumping slowly.

I zip up my raincoat, my parka,
my all-weather jacket. I brace
myself for the torrent
of words and rage he'll throw
at me. The anger raining down,
stinging my skin, invisible
cuts that will never quite heal
but will sing with pain every
time lightning strikes.

I've started seeking shelter elsewhere,
finding warmth and words from another
mouth. His hands never curl into thunder-
fists, his tongue never spins
an uncontrolled storm. I shed
my layers, find the sun in his skin,
lay content in his clear skies.

SMASH

I'm not being hyperbolic, he says,
*I literally want to smash
someone's face in.* My vision darkens,
the words *baseball bat, smash, face*
flashing in front of my eyes.

Stop staring at me, he demands
and I find a spot on the floor to study –
memorize the texture of the wood,
its high gloss.

He apologizes later, he always does.
I'm quiet the rest of the evening,
my mind careening to scenarios faster
than I can stop it – is this the part of *for worse*
that everyone suffers through?

I go to bed alone, dream of baseball bats
raining down, smashing windows and bodies,
blind to their target. I take shelter
from this storm I've seen coming,
stand quiet with arms curled around
myself.

When I wake I check the weather, peer outside
into the clear blue, wonder when the storm
will appear. I pack my bag,
leave my umbrella behind.

Mosaic

The mosaic is all black and blue,
green and red, all shattered
glass and pieced back together.

I stand staring at the mirrored
pieces, my splintered
reflection glaring back at me.

I think of the last time
I saw you, your big hand clutching
my arm, your fist smashing
the plaster beside my face,
the powdery dust rising
from the hole you left.

I packed my things, left
the mess of the drywall scattered
across the floor, a layer of fine
dust clinging to my hair,
the fingerprint bruises
mosaicking up my arm.

A Manifestation of Anger

Your anger wakes me,
the blooming purple fingerprint
bracelet you gave me pulses
as my blue-black blood pumps
to the staccato of your madness.

It's 2am,
I lie unmoving,
will my mind to stop
spinning, close my eyes and hope
for sleep but the sound of your metered
rage keeps me awake.

I watch the minutes march
forward till you, quiet
and apologetic, crawl
into bed beside me.
Your cold skin touches
mine, I pull away.

PAST LIVES

I wonder how many lives I've lived,
this cannot be the first. I wonder
if I make the same mistakes each
incarnation, if every time I'm seduced by his
hands, his mouth, his easy lies. If every
time I quit school and leave
the country, following that same
man. Does he break me in every
life? Do I live in the same version
of the same town that I hate? Do I stay
there for nine years each life, caught
in his grasp till a restraining order creates
a gap wide enough to slip through?
Maybe future me can travel back
to previous me and give guidance.
Perhaps future me can convince
current me to let him go, walk away,
move on. Perhaps past me can
remind me I've made these mistakes
before. Perhaps current me could listen.

On Asking a Friend if She Will Be My Safe House

Everyone understands the blooming
of a bruise, the sunsetting
across a cheek, the swollen
eye or busted lip. Few understand
the violence of words without fists,
the terror of vocabulary.

I have to explain, to insist – he doesn't
touch me, he's never hit me
but even as I say this it's hard to believe.
Even if my skin never
bore the bruise of his hand
my psyche blooms
with a yellow-green-blue shadow
that never completely fades.

She drops the key into my open
hand. We drink more wine, talk
of other things. She eyes
me over her glass, searches
my exposed skin for bruises.
She'll never find any, I'd leave
if he hit me.

FENCE

You came back to tear down
the fence –
it was half-falling, rotted,
a danger.

I thought it safe to go to work,
to leave you
to the physical labor,
to trust you
wouldn't repeat previous mistakes.

When I returned home
the fence was gone, a pile
of rotten wood lay
heaped in the backyard.

In the bedroom I found
my journal left open
to the page you found
most offensive.
You'd scrawled SLUT
across the page
in large red letters.

I wondered where you'd
found the red pen
or if you'd taken to carrying
one with you should the
opportunity to shame me
present itself.

I paid a friend to haul
away the warped wood
and build a new fence,
the smell of sawdust
filling my yard for days.

I Should Have Said

When you flipped
on the light, blanketed
our bedroom with brightness
after you'd read the emails
between him and me.

When I baked
a cake and texted another and you
played video games till 3am.

When you shoved
the coffee table, sent my collection
of sea glass swimming, bits of blue and green,
a tsunami swirling around us.

When you read my diary,
learned the names of every boy
and every girl I'd ever kissed –
sometimes more than one
in a single day – but assured me
you still loved me anyway.

When you asked if I'd get rid
of the dog when you moved out.
As if she were as easy to replace
as you.

I should have said *no*.

TRASH

Drunk in a bar he corners
his ex, the one who cut
his heart into paper valentines
then lit them on fire. I'm the newest
girlfriend watching the man I love
yell at the woman he still loves.
Friends drag him away, hand him
sheepishly off to me. I take him
home, force his weaving body
into the elevator, into his apartment.
He stumbles, knocks a picture off
the wall. He collapses on the couch
while I sweep the tiny pieces
into the garbage. The next day
he apologizes, tells me he loves me.
I mention the shattered glass, my heart.
He looks confused, tells me he took the trash
out this morning. *Yes,* I smile, *you did.*

LANDFILL

I still have my wedding
ring. Divorced nearly
a decade but that small
circle of gold and diamonds still
sits at the bottom of my jewelry box,
a landfill of random color and metal
and plastic. Occasionally I pull it out,
slip it onto my finger, always surprised
it still fits – as if it shouldn't somehow
since you no longer fit me.
I don't know what to do with it. I can't
throw it away, though once I was tempted
to bury it, to return the metal and stones
back to the earth. For now it lies
silent, a quiet testament to what was,
an occasional reminder that diamonds
are forever, even if we weren't.

Upon Reading the Words "Time Capsule" and Remembering

we created one.
It was early, we still felt
like newlyweds, even though
we technically weren't – still held
hands when we walked, still kissed
each night before falling asleep.
We had just gotten the backyard
regraded to prevent the basement
from flooding from the water
runoff during the heavy rains
that plagued us that summer
and we were laying a stone
patio – huge pieces of slate
that I couldn't lift. We decided
to make a time capsule, to bury
it under the corner of the patio,
beneath the gravel and a square
stone. I don't remember what we
included in it. I wonder if anyone
has found it, opened it, examined
the artifact of our love. I wonder
if they think we're still happy.

TINY CHUNKS

Why, ten years after our divorce was finalized,
am I remembering the nickname we gave your balls?
Ben and Matt, after Ben Affleck and Matt Damon.
I don't remember the context behind the joke only
that we found it hilarious and it stuck. Why is this
what pops into my head when I haven't held your hand,
much less your balls, in a decade? Our relationship
distilled into tiny chunks of memory that can be called
up or pushed aside. I don't remember
your proposal or our vows just that we broke
them. I remember the secret friendships I kept, afraid
of the jealousy you fed like a hungry pet. And when you
discovered the man emailing me you unleashed it, calling
me *whore, slut, cunt.* I don't remember our anniversary
or the first time I said *I love you* but I remember the way
you spread your arms and shouted *Is this not enough
for you?* then careened out the door. I remember sitting
in the courtroom listening to the woman tell the judge
that her companion *needed to call before he came over*
and wanting to laugh but couldn't because you were sitting
on the other side, waiting your turn to talk, to fight
the restraining order I'd taken out against you
when you'd shouted *I'll come into the fucking house and take
what's mine! I'll take what I'm goddamn owed – you'll get
what's coming to you!* I couldn't laugh, couldn't look at you
and when the judge's gavel dropped I knew how completely
I had severed us.

As Instructed

He instructs us to write a letter
to someone telling them of the thing
that would change our lives forever.
I write to you, confess
my uncertainties, my not-quite-love,
write it's over, write I'm sorry,
so sorry. Sign my name.
We address our letters, fold
them. He collects them, piles
them on the table at the front
of the room. I watch the messy
stack of paper as he lectures.
At the end of class he lays
a hand on the stack, tells us
this thing we've written, this secret
we've confessed, this thing many
of us admitted to being terrified
of – we needed to write about it.
Then he lets us collect our letters
and leave. I tuck mine
into my pocket, forget about it.
You find it three days later.

BEAUTIFUL

You never tell me I'm beautiful.
No, that's not exactly true
and it's not fair if I make you
out to be a monster.
You rarely tell me I'm beautiful.
It's become something
I track, like a young girl
tracking her period, trying to predict
when it will come again, when it's safe
to wear her new, white shorts,
show off her long, tan, beautiful legs.

TIDE

We sit talking, our beers sweating
in front of us. She reminds me
we had this same conversation
five years ago. *Really?* I ask.
She nods slowly and the memory rises
over me, the water rushing in.
How I complained
of his temper, how unhappy I was
but unable to express it, how words
were marbles in my mouth – I tried
to talk around them without any falling
out. We sip our beers in silence,
look out over the water that surrounds
her house, watch the tide slowly
come in.

STARS

I used to think the stars were keeping track:
one for every time I said no,
one for every hole he punched,
one for the police called,
one for the restraining order,
one for every drink I had that night,
one for the flowers dying in the murky water,
one for the plane ticket,
one for the apology,
one for his name blinking on my phone,
one for the bruised cheek,
one for the busted lip,
one for walking away,
one for starting over,
one for the homemade lasagna,
one for the wine,
one for the summer thunderstorms,
one for the late nights,
one for the lies,
one for the wishes made when the candles
get blown out.

END OF A RELATIONSHIP

Yesterday, which more or less lasted
seven years, we sat across from one another,
coffee cups between us as the first line
of defense.

We chose a public place to conduct
the final severing – the handing over
of scattered objects after departure.

Eight months ago you left,
your suitcase sitting patiently
by the door. Your ring, that pale
circle of silver, dropped into the jar
of sea glass I kept on the end table.
Four weeks later, the locks changed,
the restraining order served.

I handed over a paper bag, stuffed
full of you. My naked
hands shook when I lifted the coffee
to my lips. You pretended
not to notice – you'd perfected
not-noticing. For once I appreciated it.

Two days later, I walked into
that same coffee shop and right
into your girlfriend. She startled
before shuffling quickly past.

I ordered a coffee, large instead
of the usual small.
My hands didn't shake at all.

FULL

OCEAN

I've got insomnia
again. I lie awake
for hours, listening
to the fan whirl
as my thoughts swim
round and round to you.
You're six hours
behind so when I can't
sleep we text, the quiet
pinging of your incoming
message the whale song
I listen for. We tread
carefully but each message
has an undercurrent. We wade
deeper into these waters, aware
of the rip tide threatening below.
I split my life between two
oceans, split my body between
two pairs of hands – floating
toward the current, my heart
underwater, the hands
capable of saving
or drowning me.

AFLOAT

We lie heaving, sweat still
sticking to our salty skin. Our breath
slows and I begin dragging
my nails lightly across his back –
sometimes tracing the tattoos
that swirl across his shoulders
and cascade down his spine,
sometimes writing messages
he will never decipher.

This island is our sanctuary,
the only place we exist.
I draw maps on his skin,
write love letters the tide
will wash away. We are not
safe in our cathedral of sand
but still we worship
one another here, oblivious
to the relentlessly crashing
waves.

We sleep curled together, his body
forming a question mark around me,
all the things he hasn't asked
blanketing us.

Eventually I'll leave, fly
above the blue quilt of water
and return to dry land. He'll stay
behind, my tears mixing
with ocean, holding him afloat.

FUTURE FATE

It is not love that glides
my hand across his body
like the heart of a Ouija
board pushing toward fate.
Like the cosmic forces neither
of us believe in that pull us
closer – my lips to his lips,
my hips to his. The fortune
in my cookie advised,
Make decisions slowly.
His declared, A*n exciting
time is in store for you.*
I crumpled the tiny paper
in my hand. Kissed
him for the first time.
He takes my hand,
opens my palm. *Reading
my future?* I ask, smiling
into the curve where his
shoulder meets his neck.
He says nothing, just
traces the lines and kisses
my palm, sealing our fate.

DROWN

He wraps his arms around me
and holds me till I fall asleep.

Last night I slept for almost
six hours, the longest
I've slept in weeks. He is happy
I didn't wake till 4:30, happy
I finally felt safe enough
to sleep beside him.

I don't tell him I dreamt
of drowning, of him on the shore,
with my other. My other holding
him back as he tried to save me.

I wake gulping for air,
try to forget
the dream, try to forget
the taste of salt water flooding
my mouth and nose.

The next day we go to the beach,
While he reclines on a blanket,
I swim slowly into the turquoise
water, my eyes on him
the entire time.

FLYING

The wheels spin beneath us
and then, the whoosh of air
as we lift off, tires tucking
into the plane's belly
as we climb into the clouds.
The sun sets behind us
as we ascend, moving further
into darkness as we shoot
forward in the atmosphere. I left
you behind, the sun still
setting on your face as you
watched my plane disappear.
You've asked for no promises
but I still feel the ache
of wanting to give you everything
as I watch the island grow
small below me. I wonder
how long you stood
watching the sky, following
the plane with your eyes till
it was a spot against
the darkening blue that disappeared
when you blinked.

TAN

I stand naked in front
of a mirror. My hands
skim the tan lines
that curve down my body,
the lines he follows
with his fingers, his mouth.
I know when I leave this island oasis
my flesh will grow paler each day.
I wonder if he, too, will fade
from my body, if each day
I will remember
    less and less
till he's only a ghost of a freckle
against my skin.

FULL

The moon is full –
a nightlight glowing
pale in the sky.

I used to look at it
and think of a man
I had an affair with – a brief
but not disastrous affair. Just
uneventful...he never
made me cum.

Now I think of the ocean surging
toward my new lover, his toes
in the water, his hands
in my hair. I can't
smell the ocean without tasting
his tongue, I can't look
at the moon without feeling
his hands on my skin.

We glow in the bright moon-
light, the curtains flung
open, the balcony we fucked
on earlier awash in pale
light. He sleeps beside me,
quiet and content. I stare
at the dark sky, wondering
if we'll still be together
for the next full moon.

SALT WATER HAIBUN

On my last day there he calls, tells me we're going on an adventure. I throw my clothes into my suitcase and head his way.

The sun is blinding,
blue skies stretch infinitely,
trees verdant and bright.

He gets in, towel in hand, directs me into traffic. He doesn't say where we're going and I don't ask. Twenty minutes later we arrive. *We're going into the Mermaid Caves*, he says.

Water pummeled rock,
the sea surging, careful –
one must check the tides.

He lowers himself into the water, through the hole in the ground. I can see the waves crashing, the glittering sun through the water and I follow. We wade further into this strange watery world. When he boosts me finally out of the hole, I kiss his salty lips.

Relentless waves roll,
the ocean never stopping,
no mermaids appear.

BURN

I sit in front of the fire, the wood so dry
it pops, embers rain out, a small burn
marks the rug, evidence
of the offense.

When I met him the spark glowed hot.
How quickly I reacted, knowing to let it smolder
could mean a home in flames. I don't
always do this, extinguish the fires that burn
low, snuff out the desires before they can rage,
burning everything to the ground.

By the end of winter the rug is filled with tiny
black holes, embers leaving their mark,
a reverse constellation. By the end of winter
I have let desire burn hot enough to melt
all reason.

SELF-PORTRAIT WITH & WITHOUT

With soy milk. With a latte drunk
each morning in the dark kitchen. Without
the lights on because you slept on the couch
again and I don't want to wake you. With dinner
with friends, everything fine. Without conversation
during the car ride back. With negotiations
as to who walks the dog when we get home. With you
in front of the computer when I go to bed. Without
the weight of you beside me. Without my rings
on when I sleep because my fingers swell. With them on
the next day, newly cleaned and brilliant. With
the sun prisming off the diamonds as I drive
to work. With me spinning them around as I fly, my fingers
puffy by the time I land. Without them on when I shower
away the day's grime. With my hands bare as I open the door
and let him in. With my hands on him. Without a word said.

RIOT IN MY THROAT

After the toasts have been made
and mouths kissed and champagne
swallowed we state our resolutions –
the usuals are all there: exercise
more, drink less (and we toast
again), save more, spend less. I can't
voice my resolution, can't tell my friends
that I resolve to give you up. Only 8%
of New Year's resolutions are kept, most fail
by February. These numbers mingle
with the champagne in my mouth.
I swallow them both, fight to keep
them down, a riot in my throat.

CUT

First I cut / off my hands so I couldn't / touch / him, couldn't hold him. When this wasn't / enough I cut off / my ears so I couldn't hear / him whisper, *Good morning / beautiful.* Next I cut / off my lips, my tongue, removed / my ability to kiss / him, to hold / his name / in my mouth. When none / of these helped, when I still / felt the dull ache / for him, when he still haunted / my dreams I finally / plunged the blade / into my chest and cut / out my heart – a glistening, wet / muscle that echoed his name with each / beat. It pounded / wildly and then stopped, shuttered / to silence, his name / finally cut / from me.

CATCH AND RELEASE

It took his father dying to break us. He didn't tell
me immediately, instead reeled out this
information slowly, a fisherman setting the bait
and I opened my mouth, bit what was offered,
felt the sharp tug of the hook against my lip.
First he told me he couldn't see me
when I arrived – we'd been apart
for two months, been planning our reunion
for weeks. *Why?* I asked. *I'll see you on the 29th*
he said. Eventually he tells me
his father has died, then doesn't speak
to me for seven days, the hook in my lip
festering. I don't know what it's like
to lose a parent, to suddenly be orphaned –
perhaps talking to your lover is too much to ask
while grieving. Perhaps it was only
a game of catch and release.

I Guess We'll Have to be Secretly in Love

To pull back, to not call
you *love*
    or *lover* or *gorgeous.*
To not   tangle –
my hands in your hair, my legs
    in your legs. To not send
you birthday wishes
    (which you hate to celebrate
        but I love),
or a Christmas gift   wrapped
in candy cane wrapping paper
    (which I hate to celebrate
    but you love).
To walk backwards
        out of the ocean,
to not feel the sand being pulled
back from under our feet.
    To not
feel like drowning.
To not smile
        at your painted
toes. To say *I love you*
to another name.   To not even
    think
your name but keep it under
my tongue,
      like a pill
        I cannot allow
myself to swallow.
        To not share
sushi or champagne –
to eat the whole
    plate/drink
the whole bottle
      myself.
To watch the days march
            forward
without the ability
    to freeze

time, to freeze
　　　　this moment,
to freeze
the way you look
at me　　　　　in the morning.
To not have your brow furrow
　　when you realize
I haven't slept. To never
　　sleep
again, to never hear
your heavy　breath
or feel your arm　　reach
for me in the dark.
　　For sunrise to never
come, for the sun to stop
　　　　setting
behind the palm trees, to never
watch
　　the ocean swallow it.
To not remember
　　your tattoo
under my lips, to not trace
　　　　a path
with my fingertips.
To not breathe
　　the same air as you.
To not breathe.
To not.

If Certain Physicists Are Correct, There are Infinite Universes

If they're right, then I believe one exists
where we're together – where your hand
reaches out each morning and finds my body,
solid beside you in bed, the sun just peeking
through. If there's another universe we hold hands
in it and I don't scan the crowds to see if someone
I know is watching. In that universe your mouth
meets mine, and all I think about is the urgency
of your tongue. Still the green trees and blooming
flowers, the wind tangling my hair. But in that universe
it's salt water and an ocean breeze and your tattooed
arms pulling me close as another wave surges over us.
In that universe we drive with the top down every day,
point out rainbows when they appear. If there's another
universe you are still you and he is still he and I am still
me but in this universe I'm with him and in that universe
I'm with you. In another universe I don't have to worry
about whose heart I'm going to break.

BEAUTIFUL

GUILTY

I look like an unloved wife – brilliant
diamonds circle my finger, promise
vows my heart is still trying to keep.
In hotel bars men buy me drinks and hope
for a night between my thighs.
Sometimes I let them
lean close, fingers grazing
my warm skin. My lips brush
their cheek before telling them
no. I leave with only their names
clutched between my teeth,
go to bed naked
but alone, feel guilty
for crimes I've not yet
committed.

COMING HOME

Over dinner he asks, *who will leave first?*
He's joking but my heart still drops a bit.
It'll be you, he continues, *I've got nothing*
better lined up. I smile, laugh, sip my wine —
all too aware of my wandering eyes, my fickle
heart. I could fall in love a million times a day
but I keep coming home to him, keep crushing
the crushes, keep shoving hands in pockets
to keep from pulling another close.

GOOD LIVES

I wake the next morning,
fingers still smelling of myself,
your words still in my ear.

You wouldn't come
in last night, wouldn't park
your car and follow me inside.

You said you wanted us –
both of us to have good lives
and if you came to my room
we wouldn't be able to turn away
from the path tempting us.

When I return to my good life
I take your voice in my ear, all the things
we didn't do circling in my head.

2AM

knows all my secrets –
how I wake and look
at the clock, knowing
sleep is over for me,
how he reaches out
and pulls me
close, as if he could
pull me into his dream.

I wonder how long
this will last – the insomnia,
this relationship. I curl into
him, my body an ampersand
to his. I lie cocooned by him
till the alarm I don't need
begins to blare.

The next morning he comments
on how little I sleep. He wants me
to fall into dreams the way
he does, his whole body
relaxing into darkness.

I try but each night
I fail and each night
he reaches for me, plants
kisses on my skin, holds
me so even if I can't
sleep, I can't help but think
maybe, maybe this could last.

BREAK

We were standing in my kitchen,
close and I could almost feel
your breath against my breath.
Neither of us moved, my hand
frozen in the air halfway between
us, hesitating. The moment shattered
when the wine bottle slipped
from my other hand,
glass and red grenading
across the tile.
You stepped back carefully,
reached for a towel, began cleaning up.
I stood stock-still, the shards glittering
against my bare feet as you gently
wiped the glass from my skin, each touch
a reminder of how
we could break one another.

NUMBERS

He suggests we renew
our vows, even though
we've been married
only three years. I don't
tell him I once read
that couples who renew
their vows almost always
get divorced. We don't
need another statistic
against us. Already
50% of marriages end.
This is my second
marriage so the odds
are worse, there's a
67% chance it won't work.
My husband is a scientist,
a lover of numbers
and data. I am a poet
yet I'm the one plagued
by these facts. I play
with the numbers,
adjust the ratios
and change the percentages,
hope our numbers
improve and we have
a chance.

EVEN THOUGH WE'RE NO LONGER TOGETHER

I still calculate the time
difference, still do the backward
math to determine if you're awake,
if you've read my text, if you're
at work or at the gym. I still remember
the solid weight of you in my bed,
the way you reached for me as I lay
unsleeping. Still scroll through
pictures, find the few I have –
us on the water, squinting against
the island sun. Us leaning close,
heads tilted toward one another as though
conspiring for a future we know we won't
have. I still want you to call me
beautiful, still want you to miss me, still want you
to want me. I still sent you a birthday
card, the perfect balance of caring
and not caring. I calculated the days,
did the backward math, mailed
the card a week early, still hoping
it arrived in time.

NEST

The hummingbird's wings
tickle my bones, flutter
against my ribs, remind
me of the empty
I keep inside, reserved
for him. When he slips
his hands between
my collar bones, reaches
into my throat without
crushing my voice I feel
him touch the tiny bird,
pet her softly. He could crush
her but instead he creates
a nest with his palms, the bird
settling in, preening her colors
for him.

MY FRIEND OFFERS TO READ MY CARDS

and immediately, upon pulling two from the stack, says, *Fuck.*
Bad? I ask, though obviously it is. *An obstacle and a path,*
she replies, laying the cards face up so I can read them.
The Firefly is the first card, the obstacle, and it tells me
the high-frequency cannot be sustained, that there is Firefly
energy behind every poem, that harnessing this energy
is vital yet potentially destructive. The next card, the path,
is The Hummingbird: the ability to find energy and positivity
and return to it every day. We both sit back, thoughts swarming.
So what does this mean? Related to my question? I ask.
She frowns, uncertain of the interpretation. Finally she asks,
What do you think? I pause, moving words around in my mouth,
unsure where to begin. *I think I write poems about the destruction,*
to try to keep it at bay, to keep the monster in the closet. I pause,
my mouth suddenly dry. *And I think I have to find joy that I can have*
every day. That I'm not constantly fighting for. She nods, agreeing.

She knows of the broken bones and busted
plaster. She knows of the eggshells that line
the floors of my home. She doesn't know
of the one whose soft words fill my ears,
how my fear melts away when I'm with him.

I have a lot to think about, I finally say.
She nods and reshuffles the deck.

SUPER BLUE BLOOD MOON
"Everyone is a moon and has a dark side which they never show to anyone."
– Mark Twain

There's a full moon tonight – a super blue blood
moon which just means it's huge and violet-
tinged. You're flying, every minute brings you closer
to me. I wonder if you'll see the moon from your window,
bigger from your bird's eye view. I don't remember
such things in years past but maybe that's part
of her charm – her ability to keep us hooked and wanting
more. I watch the moon as I drive to the airport.
We embrace when you arrive, you shove your hands
into my hair, pull me close. The moon watches.

PAST LOVER

Past lover looks at his phone, thinks
of texting her but doesn't, places it back
in his pocket, waits for a vibration to notify
him a message has arrived. Not from her
though, never from her anymore.

Past lover buys chicken, broccoli, carrots
and onion. Roasts them. Sits at an empty
table and eats quietly. Wonders if she's
eating, what she's eating, who she's eating with.

Past lover stretches the hammock between
trees, watching the ocean slowly devour
the sun, remembers when they lay
here together.

Past lover lies down after a long day, looks
at the clock, does the math. They are literally
a world apart, an ocean between them, her day
just starting as his ends. He thinks of calling,
good morning beautiful. Doesn't.

Past lover sees a rainbow, snaps a picture,
posts it online because he can't send
it to her. The plumeria are blooming.
She was here this time last year.

SHIPWRECK

This heart sank years
ago, the demon-pirates
pulling it down to the blue-black
depths, algae and coral
making their home in its echoing
chambers.

I keep chipping away
at the shipwreck of my heart,
keep finding treasures
I assumed I'd lost or maybe
never had. His hands
on my skin —
    treasure,
how he calls me beautiful
a dozen times a day —
     treasure.

Now I think of raising my heart,
of the masts filling again,
of sailing on his voice,
his hands, the breeze
of his body.

Mood

I always loved mood
rings as a child, it was the treasure
I chose at the dentist, the prize
I purchased from the gumball
machine that sat in grocery store entries.
I would slip the cheap silver band
onto my finger and press it close
to my skin - I wanted every degree
of body heat to register.
Red was in love, green was envy, blue
was happy. Every time my ring refused
to change, stayed a stubborn
black. How I wished, just once, that the stone
would turn red – obsessed, even then,
with knowing if I was in love.

STILL

We sat side by side, a feather
of air between us, the first time
together in months. I wondered
if you were imagining the salt
of my tongue, the bite
of my skin, the low of my moan.
We spent hours
together, talking but never
touching until
we said goodbye at 2am.
I held you then, my breath
kissed your skin as I whispered,
Still.

WEATHER / LOVE

We trade weather reports like love
letters – you send a picture of the aquamarine
sky behind the verdant mountains that rise
up from the ocean, your smile in the middle
of the frame. I can almost smell the salt
water breeze as it tangles your hair. I respond
with a photo, my smile as bright as my umbrella
against the concrete sky.

It's been raining for ten days – I crave sunshine
and your hands. You send a photo of a rainbow.
I recognize the street you live on, remember
each time I parked, walked into your house,
crawled into your bed.

There's a thunderstorm tonight, loud
and bright. I sleep with the blinds open, watch
the lightning flash through the window. I tell
you I'm naked in bed, the room illuminated
with each crack. I can't photograph the flash,
the lightning moving too quick for me to capture.
I send you a photo of my body instead, my skin
pale against the dark sheets. *I wish
you were here*, I say, knowing we'd fuck
hard and fast, the percussion of the storm
our soundtrack.

The next morning dawns clear and bright,
the storm pulling the clouds with it as it moves
up the coast, the azure sky a welcome
sight. The emerald grass sodden, the seeds
of desire pushing through the earth,
growing wild.

FADING

You are fading
from my body, the feel
of your hands ghosting,
the memory of you burning
off as the sun slowly climbs the sky.
I expected it to be painful,
to rip you from my thoughts, cut a hole
in my heart and pull you from it, bloody
and pulsing. Instead you are the echo
of a heartbeat. I thought I would need
black magic to rid your memory
from my skin but it seems I've shed
you already, the carcass
of you sloughing off
with the lightest touch. I leave you,
your touch, the way you held
my name in your mouth.

LEGEND

You lie sleeping beside me, arm heavy
across my body, breathing steady.
A Japanese legend says if you can't
sleep it's because you're awake
in someone else's dream. I wonder
if it's your dream that holds me
captive, if we're together,
free and happy in a way we don't
exist in the waking world. I count
backwards, ease into sleep, and dream
of an endless hallway with dozens
of doors, each an opportunity
but none contain you.

PEARL

I hold your memory like sand
on my tongue – the heat
of your hands on my skin,
the sound of my name
on your lips – and wonder
if I should swallow.
Or let it linger in my mouth
till a pale pearl emerges,
to be worn like a talisman
at the base of my throat.

How to Survive Heartbreak

Acknowledge the wrecking
ball in your chest, the slow
heaving back
and forth as it crashes
against your heart.
Brush your teeth
but avoid
the mirror. Drape it with black
cloth. Wail
your prayers, drop
to your knees, touch
lips to the ground
to remember
you're here.
Take fistfuls of dirt,
fill your pockets, fill
your mouth, plant
seeds and add water. Wait
for flowers to bloom.
Tilt your face
to the sun, let the warm
be the only thing that matters.
Throw away
your calendar and your watch.
Stay awake
till the stars come out.
If you can't see
the stars, drive deep
into the country till they explode
in the sky. Lie on your back.
Feel the cool grass, hear
the crickets, know the empty
place inside you is not
as infinite as the universe.
Fill the void in your chest
with stars
and rocks and blades of grass.

ACKNOWLEDGEMENTS & NOTES

Thank you to Freddy for believing in this manuscript and giving it a home
with Vegetarian Alcoholic Press. Thank you to my MFA sister-wives, Sita
and Whitney: your friendship, support, and motherfucking pep talks have
saved me time and again. Thanks to my sister, Kirsten, and my best friend,
Virginia, for always believing in me. Thank you to my mentor, Cathy – you
are my favorite tomato. And a huge thank you to my husband, Jay, who
doesn't always like what I write but never asks me to stop. I love you so
much, you are my person.

The poet kindly thanks the following journals which first gave her poems a
home, sometimes in earlier forms:

Babe Soda: Forest Fire
Queen of Cups: Bucket Heart
bloodsugar poetry: Past Lives, Drown
The Green Light: Rewind
NoVa Bards Anthology: A Manifestation of Anger
Rogue Poetry Review: Fence
Bound: If Only
Dandelion Review: I Should Have Said
Door = Jar: Trash
Sad Girl Review: Tiny Chunks
Vending Machine Press: Stars, How to Survive Heartbreak
Bourgeon: Ocean
Anti-Heroin Chic: Afloat, 2am
New Southern Fugitives: Future Fate, Even Though We're No Longer
   Together
Cauldron Anthology: Seasons: Tan, Riot in My Throat, My Friend Offers to
   Read My Cards
TERSE Journal: Salt Water Haibun, Burn
Riggwelter Press: Self-Portrait With & Without
former cactus: Cut
Flypaper Magazine: Catch and Release
Mojave Heart Journal: If Certain Physicists Are Correct, There are Infinite
   Universes
Broadkill Review: Guilty
Milk + Beans: Coming Home
Bone & Ink Press: Legend
Gemstone Patio: Pearl

The Violence Within, a chapbook containing several of these poems, was published by *Flutter Press* in February 2018.

The first line of "Forest Fire" was inspired by the poem "Operation: Get Down" by Alex Lemon.

Part of the opening line in "End of a Relationship" is borrowed from "End of a Friendship" by Frank Bidart.

The first line of "Future Fate" is borrowed from "The Smell of Sex" by Jeff Walt.

"I Guess We'll Have to be Secretly in Love" was inspired by a poem by Rosebud Ben-Oni with the same title.

"Guilty" borrows lines from "thousands" by Lightsey Darst.

Courtney LeBlanc is the author of *Beautiful & Full of Monsters* (*Vegetarian Alcoholic Press*), chapbooks *All in the Family* (*Bottlecap Press*) and *The Violence Within* (*Flutter Press*), and a Pushcart Prize nominee. She has her MBA from University of Baltimore and her MFA from Queens University of Charlotte. She loves nail polish, wine, and tattoos. Read her publications on her blog: www.wordperv.com. Follow her on twitter: @wordperv, and IG: @wordperv79.

* 9 7 8 0 5 7 8 6 2 5 9 5 9 *